I0896291

Greatest of All Time College Sports

G.O.A.T. College Men's Basketball Players

Beth Adelman

Lerner Publications ◆ Minneapolis

Stats in this book are accurate through the 2023–2024 men's college basketball season.

Copyright © 2026 by Lerner Publishing Group, Inc.

All rights reserved. International copyright secured. No part of this book may be reproduced, stored in a retrieval system, or transmitted in any form or by any means—electronic, mechanical, photocopying, recording, or otherwise—without the prior written permission of Lerner Publishing Group, Inc., except for the inclusion of brief quotations in an acknowledged review.

Lerner Publications Company
An imprint of Lerner Publishing Group, Inc.
241 First Avenue North
Minneapolis, MN 55401 USA

For reading levels and more information, look up this title at www.lernerbooks.com.

Main body text set in Aptifer Sans LT Pro.
Typeface provided by Linotype.

Library of Congress Cataloging-in-Publication Data

Names: Adelman, Beth, author.
Title: G.O.A.T. college men's basketball players / Beth Adelman.
Other titles: GOAT college men's basketball players
Description: Minneapolis, MN : Lerner Publications, [2026] | Series: Greatest of all time college sports (Lerner sports) | Includes bibliographical references and index. | Audience: Ages 7–11 | Audience: Grades 2–3 | Summary: "Men's college basketball players bring the excitement with high-flying dunks, long three-pointers, and buzzer-beating baskets. But who are the best players of all time? Meet them, review their stats, and then make your own list"—Provided by publisher.
Identifiers: LCCN 2024044928 (print) | LCCN 2024044929 (ebook) | ISBN 9798765668573 (library binding) | ISBN 9798765684191 (paperback) | ISBN 9798765677810 (epub)
Subjects: LCSH: Basketball players—Rating of—United States—Juvenile literature. | College athletes—Rating of—United States—Juvenile literature. | College sports—Juvenile literature. | Basketball—United States—History—Juvenile literature.
Classification: LCC GV885.1 .A334 2026 (print) | LCC GV885.1 (ebook) | DDC 796.323—dc23/eng/20250110

LC record available at https://lccn.loc.gov/2024044928
LC ebook record available at https://lccn.loc.gov/2024044929

Manufactured in the United States of America
1-1011968-53825-4/24/2025

TABLE OF CONTENTS

Christian Laettner makes a game-winning shot against Kentucky.

Buzzer-Beater!

There were 2.1 seconds left in overtime during the 1992 men's NCAA basketball tournament. Duke University was trailing the University of Kentucky 103–102. Duke's Grant Hill threw a pass far down the court to teammate Christian Laettner. Laettner hadn't missed a shot all night. He faked right, dribbled once, turned, and hit the winning jump shot as the final buzzer sounded! Nine days later, Duke beat Michigan to become the national champion.

Almost 100 years earlier, on February 9, 1895, Minnesota State School of Agriculture sent a basketball team to Hamline University in Saint Paul, Minnesota. It was the first college basketball game. Minnesota State won 9–3.

Between that first game and Duke's victory in 1992, many college basketball rules had changed. That makes it hard to compare players over time. For example, until 1972, freshmen couldn't play on varsity college teams. In modern college basketball, freshman can play right away.

Shot clocks make basketball more exciting for fans, but they weren't part of the college game until 1985.

FACTS AT A GLANCE

- Stephen Curry made 41 percent of his shots from three-point range in his college career.
- The NCAA banned slam dunks between 1967 and 1976. This was meant to slow down tall players such as Kareem Abdul-Jabbar.
- Only two college players have racked up more than 2,000 points and 2,000 rebounds in their college careers.
- Bill Russell changed the way defense is played. He brought his talent as a track-and-field high jumper onto the basketball court.

The 45-second shot clock wasn't used until 1985. It shrank to 30 seconds by 2015. That increased scoring and made the game faster and more exciting. The three-point shot didn't count until 1986. Before then, a field goal from any distance scored only two points.

For a long time, Black players were prevented from playing on many of the best college basketball teams. Some conferences didn't allow Black players until the late 1960s. Many Black players faced racism throughout their careers.

This book includes Division I superstars who played more than one year in college. Rankings are not based on how many championships they won. They're based on players' stats and how they helped their teams play better.

You may disagree with the order of this list. You may think some great players are missing. It's fun to think about making different choices.

Fletcher Magee (left) broke NCAA Division I records with 504 career three-pointers.

NO. 10

Tyler Hansbrough slam dunks the ball during a game in 2006.

TYLER HANSBROUGH

UNIVERSITY OF NORTH CAROLINA (2005–2009)

Tyler Hansbrough was intense as a college freshman at the University of North Carolina (UNC). His game was physical. It was a mixture of hustle and chasing down rebounds. Fans called him a warrior. Opponents described him as a beast.

Hansbrough was the only freshman in Atlantic Coast Conference (ACC) history to earn First-Team All-America honors. He was also the first UNC player to lead his team in scoring, rebounding, field goal average, and steals in the same season!

Hansbrough's high-energy style caused opponents to often foul him. But fouling Hansbrough was usually a mistake, because he was the most successful player at the free throw line. He still holds the all-time men's college basketball record for most career free-throws with 982.

Hansbrough keeps his eyes on the basket as he takes a free throw.

TYLER HANSBROUGH FACTS

- Hansbrough earned First-Team All-America and First-Team All-ACC honors in each of his four college seasons. He was the first ACC player to do that.
- He was the NCAA Player of the Year in 2008. He helped make UNC national champions in 2009.
- His stready play meant his teammates could always count on him. He averaged at least 18 points and 7 rebounds per game in college.
- UNC has been to the NCAA tournament more than 50 times. They are one of the winningest college teams ever. With 325 points, Hansbrough is their all-time top scorer in NCAA tournaments.
- UNC's neighbor Duke University is UNC's biggest rival. UNC leads the matchup with a 54–53 record against Duke.

NO. 9

La Salle named its home court in honor of Tom Gola.

TOM GOLA

LA SALLE UNIVERSITY (1951–1955)

Tom Gola is the greatest rebounder in men's college basketball history. He holds the NCAA record for total rebounds at 2,201. That's 171 more than runner-up Joe Holup of George Washington University has. And Holup played 14 more games than Gola!

Gola also scored 2,462 points, making him one of the best all-around players ever. Gola was the first college player to score more than 2,000 points and grab more than 2,000 rebounds in his career.

He was 6 feet 6 (1.9 m), but he played as if he was even taller. He was a forward who could shoot, rebound, and defend. He also had the dribbling and passing skills of a guard.

Gola led La Salle to the 1952 National Invitation Tournament title. He also led them to the 1954 NCAA title. In that tournament, he was named Most Outstanding Player.

After playing at La Salle, Gola (center bottom) played ten seasons in the NBA.

TOM GOLA FACTS

- Gola has the most career double-doubles with 96.
- Many fans think his record of 48 double-doubles in a row will never be beaten.
- He averaged 20.9 points and 19 rebounds over 121 games at La Salle.
- Gola and Holup are the only two NCAA players ever to rack up more than 2,000 career points and 2,000 rebounds.

NO. 8

Bill Bradley jumps to make a basket against Cincinnati.

BILL BRADLEY

PRINCETON UNIVERSITY (1962–1965)

On the court, Bill Bradley's greatest weapon was his brain. He studied the game and learned from the greats. Then he developed his own style of play. It combined the best moves he had ever seen with his own speed, grace, and skill.

Bradley could see everything happening everywhere on the court. And he practiced for thousands of hours. That gave him a strong feel for the game. He could see what was going to happen next. Then he could put himself in position to make the perfect shot or pass.

Bradley led Princeton to the 1965 Final Four. He averaged 35 points per game to lead all scorers in the tournament. Princeton lost to Michigan. But Bradley was still named the Final Four's Most Outstanding Player.

Bradley leaps to stop an opponent from scoring during a tryout for the 1964 US Olympic team.

BILL BRADLEY FACTS

- Bradley scored 2,503 points in three seasons at Princeton. He averaged 30.2 points per game.
- He was an All-American selection every year he played. In 1965, he was named Associated Press Player of the Year.
- Princeton captured the Ivy League championship every season Bradley played.
- In 1965, Bradley won the James E. Sullivan Award as the top amateur athlete in the US. He was the first basketball player to win that honor.

NO. 7

Magic Johnson controls the ball in a 1979 NCAA Final Four game against Indiana State.

MAGIC JOHNSON

MICHIGAN STATE UNIVERSITY (1977–1979)

Earvin "Magic" Johnson was exciting to watch. He was a showman with incredible skills. He was a great passer, could handle the ball well, and had amazing court vision. He always knew where the ball was going. He was big, strong, and quick. He could make jaw-dropping plays with the ball in his hands.

Johnson was also a strong leader. Michigan State had little men's basketball success before he arrived. Yet he inspired all his teammates to play at a higher level.

Johnson played only two seasons at Michigan State, but his sophomore year is legendary. He led the team to the NCAA tournament for the second year in a row. They went all the way to the title game. It was the matchup everyone wanted to see. Michigan State defeated Indiana State and Larry Bird. Johnson was voted Most Outstanding Player of the Final Four. Later, in the National Basketball Association (NBA), Bird became Johnson's biggest rival.

Johnson grabs a rebound in a 1979 NCAA game against Pennsylvania.

MAGIC JOHNSON FACTS

- Johnson was a magical basketball player in high school too. After a triple-double when he racked up 36 points, 16 assists, and 18 rebounds, fans started calling him Magic.
- In the 1979 NCAA championship game, Johnson led his team in scoring. He had 24 points, 5 assists, and 7 rebounds. It was Michigan State's first basketball title.
- Johnson led the NCAA in total assists during both of his college seasons.
- In his two years in college, Johnson averaged 17.1 points, 7.6 rebounds, and 7.9 assists per game.

NO. 6

Larry Bird dribbles the ball in the 1979 NCAA title game against Michigan State.

LARRY BIRD

INDIANA STATE UNIVERSITY (1976–1979)

Until Larry Bird joined the team, Indiana State had never been to an NCAA Division I basketball tournament. Like most great players, he made his whole team better. Bird was a great shooter, but he had a team-first mindset. He was always looking for a teammate who had an open shot. He never hesitated to pass the ball to someone else.

After his junior year at Indiana State, Bird was picked sixth overall by the NBA's Boston Celtics. But he decided to finish college. His senior year was magical. He led Indiana State to an undefeated record of 33–0. Then they went all the way to the 1979 NCAA title game.

Although they lost the game to Magic Johnson and Michigan State, Bird was named Player of the Year. Bird played 94 career college games. His team won 81 of them.

Bird takes a shot in a 1979 game against Arkansas.

LARRY BIRD FACTS

- Bird averaged more than 30 points per game. He also averaged 13.3 rebounds and 4.6 assists.
- He played his best college game in the 1979 NCAA Final Four against DePaul University. He had 35 points, 9 assists, and 16 rebounds.
- In Bird's senior season, he was first among all college players in points, rebounds, field goals, field-goal attempts, and free throws.
- Bird was well-known for his ability to shoot from long distances. But at the time, neither the NCAA nor the NBA allowed the three-point shot. The NBA began allowing the three-pointer during Bird's first season in 1979–1980.

NO. 5

Pete Maravich dribbles to make another basket.

Pete Maravich

Louisiana State University (1967–1970)

Pete Maravich holds the record for the most career points in men's college basketball with 3,667. He played in the late 1960s when three-point shots and slam dunks were not allowed. At the time, freshmen couldn't play on the varsity team. That means he played varsity for only three seasons.

As a point guard, Maravich usually had the ball. He could pass and dribble as well as he could shoot. His between-the-legs dribbling and no-look, behind-the-back passes were legendary. He loved to take long jump shots from the right side. If three-point shots had been part of the game when he played, Maravich would have a much higher career point total.

Maravich's incredible skills made his whole team better. The Louisiana State Tigers were 3–23 the year before he joined the team. In his senior year, they finished 22–10.

Maravich moves the ball between his legs to keep it away from a defender.

PETE MARAVICH FACTS

- Maravich is ranked first, fourth, and fifth on the all-time men's list for most points scored in a season. In three different seasons, he scored 1,381, 1,148, and 1,138 points.
- He had the most games in a season with at least 50 points (10), the most games in a row with at least 50 points (3), and the most games in a career with at least 50 points (28).
- Maravich scored more than 60 points in a game four times. In 1970, he had 69 points against Alabama. That's the second-highest point total for a game in Division I history.

NO. 4

Stephen Curry is one of the best shooters in basketball history.

STEPHEN CURRY

DAVIDSON COLLEGE (2006–2009)

Stephen Curry played basketball at Davidson College, a small North Carolina school. He chose Davidson because many of the bigger basketball schools thought he wasn't tall enough to be a great college player. He was only 6 foot 2 (1.9 m). But in his first season, he proved he had one of the biggest games anywhere. He set a freshman-year NCAA record with 113 three-point baskets.

As a sophomore, he came up big again. He led Davidson to a 26–6 regular-season record and a 20–0 record in the Southern Conference. Davidson then faced Gonzaga University in the first round of the NCAA tournament. Curry's team was behind at halftime, but he scored 30 points in the second half of the game. He hit the go-ahead three-pointer with 1:04 to play. Then he sealed the win by making two free throws. It was Davidson's first NCAA tournament win since 1969.

Davidson reached the Elite Eight, the last eight teams remaining in the tournament. It was a great run for a small school playing against so many bigger basketball powerhouses.

Curry celebrates a hard-fought win over Gonzaga in the first round of the 2008 NCAA tournament.

STEPHEN CURRY FACTS

- Over three college seasons, Curry made 41 percent of his three-point attempts.
- In 2008, he set a record for three-point baskets in a single college season with 162.
- During his last season at Davidson, Curry led the team in scoring average with 28.6 points per game.
- Curry left college after three years to join the NBA. In 2022, he received his college degree from Davidson.

NO. 3

Oscar Robertson raises his arms to celebrate scoring 50 points in a game against Iowa.

OSCAR ROBERTSON

UNIVERSITY OF CINCINNATI (1957–1960)

Oscar Robertson was good at everything. He was great at making plays because he had awesome passing and dribbling skills. He was great at grabbing rebounds because of his size and toughness under the basket. And he was great at blocking shots because of his quickness, reflexes, and long arms.

He was an amazing all-around player. He led all men's college players in scoring in each of his three seasons at Cincinnati.

He was the NCAA's all-time leading scorer until Pete Maravich passed him in 1970.

Each season at Cincinnati, Robertson's rebounding and passing skills improved. It was a sign of how he became even better and kept adding more skills. While his team didn't win an NCAA title, they had their best seasons with Robertson leading the way. And he helped create a winning culture at the school that continued after he left for the NBA.

Robertson leaps to grab the ball against Kansas State in 1958.

OSCAR ROBERTSON FACTS

- Robertson had four triple-doubles in the NCAA men's tournament. That's never been matched by another player.
- Robertson led the US in scoring in his first season. He had 35.1 points and 15.2 rebounds per game. His college career averages were 33.8 points, 7.1 assists, and 15.2 rebounds per game.
- He was named the College Player of the Year every year he played.
- Every year the US Basketball Writers Association honors the best men's college basketball player with the Oscar Robertson Trophy. The winner of the NBA Western Conference Finals also gets an award called the Oscar Robertson Trophy.

NO. 2

Bill Russell performs the high jump at a track-and-field competition.

BILL RUSSELL

UNIVERSITY OF SAN FRANCISCO (1953–1956)

Bill Russell completely changed the way defense is played in basketball. When he began playing at the University of San Francisco (USF), players on defense rarely jumped. Jumping was thought to take you out of the play if the shooter faked a shot. Shooters didn't jump much either. Basketball was played mostly on the floor.

In track and field, Russell was a world-class high jumper. He put that ability to work in basketball. He used his awesome athletic skills, fancy footwork, and quick instincts to jump and block shots. In his first college game, 19-year-old Russell blocked 13 shots. Blocked shots weren't an official statistic at the time. But Russell said later that he averaged about 15 blocks per game.

He always played big in the most important games. Russell led USF to back-to-back NCAA titles in 1955 and 1956. He was named the tournament's Most Outstanding Player in 1955. In the 1956 championship game against Iowa, he had an NCAA-record 27 rebounds.

Russell holds the Most Valuable Player trophy after helping San Francisco win a tournament in 1955.

BILL RUSSELL FACTS

- Russell averaged 20.7 points and 20.3 rebounds over his college career.
- With Russell, USF had a 71–8 record, including an undefeated 29–0 season in 1956.
- After Russell graduated, he became captain of the US national basketball team. They went 8–0 in the 1956 Summer Olympics and won the gold medal.
- After an outstanding pro career, Russell became the NBA's first Black head coach.

NO. 1

Kareem Abdul-Jabbar takes a shot over the outstretched arms of a defender.

Kareem Abdul-Jabbar

University of California, Los Angeles (1966–1969)

Kareem Abdul-Jabbar was a basketball legend at Power Memorial High School in New York City. He led his team to a 71-game winning streak and three state titles. He racked up 2,067 points and more than 2,000 rebounds. Both were New York City records.

He had size, quickness, agility, and a deep understanding of the game. And he went on to become the greatest college basketball player of all time. When he started at the University of California, Los Angeles (UCLA),, his name was Lew Alcindor. But he changed to Kareem Abdul-Jabbar in 1968.

When Abdul-Jabbar made up his mind to score, he was nearly unstoppable. He could shoot with both hands. And he had perfected all kinds of different shots: tip-ins, layups, jump shots, and hook shots. He was a great passer too.

Abdul-Jabbar was also the first king of the slam dunk. At 7 foot 2 (2.1 m), he could slam the ball over most defenders. After his first season at UCLA, the NCAA banned the dunk. They thought the shot gave tall players such as Abdul-Jabbar an unfair advantage. It wasn't allowed again until 1976.

Abdul-Jabbar* (left) *and UCLA head coach John Wooden celebrate their 1967 NCAA title win.

KAREEM ABDUL-JABBAR FACTS

- In the 1960s, college freshmen could not play on the varsity team. Abdul-Jabbar's first college game was a matchup between his freshmen team and the varsity squad. The freshmen won 75–60. Abdul-Jabbar had 31 points and 21 rebounds.
- In his first varsity season, he averaged 29 points and 15.5 rebounds per game.
- In all three of his varsity seasons, he was chosen the NCAA tournament's Most Outstanding Player, an All-American, and the National Player of the Year.
- UCLA won the NCAA championship every season Abdul-Jabbar played. They had a three-year record of 88–2, including a 47-game winning streak.

YOUR G.O.A.T.

Basketball is an exciting and beautiful game. There's something in it for everyone. But fans have their favorite players and moves. They might have different opinions about what makes a great basketball player. One fan's G.O.A.T. may not be another fan's G.O.A.T.

It's time to grab a sheet of paper and write down your own list. What do you think are the most important things to consider? Would you keep some of the players we picked? Would you put them in a different order? Would you choose new players?

Do you want to learn more about some of the players in this book? Find books and other resources about great basketball players of the past and present. Who will be on your G.O.A.T. top 10 list? There are no right or wrong answers. It's up to you!

MEN'S COLLEGE BASKETBALL FACTS

- Larry Bird and Magic Johnson were the two best college basketball players in 1979. They met in the most-watched men's college basketball game in history. More than 35 million people watched Indiana State take on Michigan State in the NCAA title game. Michigan State won 75–64.

- Carmelo Anthony spent just one season at Syracuse University. In 2003, he averaged 22 points and 10 rebounds per game. The freshman helped the school win their only NCAA title.

- Kevin Durant also played just one season of college basketball. But his 2006 season at the University of Texas was one of the best. With his silky-smooth jump shot, Durant averaged 29.2 points and 12.2 rebounds. And he shot 46.8 percent from three-point range.

GLOSSARY

All-American: an honor given to an amateur athlete who's one of the best in their sport

conference: a group of teams that play against one another

Division I: the highest level of NCAA sports competition

double-double: when a player reaches at least 10 in two different stats categories in a game

field goal: a made basket while the ball is in play

free throw: an open shot taken from behind a set line after a foul by an opponent

jump shot: a shot made by jumping into the air and releasing the ball with one or both hands at the peak of the jump

NCAA: National Collegiate Athletic Association, the group that oversees college sports in the United States

rebound: taking control of the ball after a missed shot

slam dunk: a shot made by jumping high into the air and throwing the ball down through the basket

LEARN MORE

Barnes, Derrick. *Basketball: Amazing but True Stories!* New York: Workman Publishing, 2023.

The College Basketball Experience: Hall of Fame
https://collegebasketballexperience.com/hall-of-fame/

NCAA: Men's Basketball
https://www.ncaa.com/sports/basketball-men/d1

Reeves, Diane Lindsey. *G.O.A.T. Women's College Basketball Teams.* Minneapolis: Lerner Publications, 2026.

Stabler, David. *Stephen Curry vs. Magic Johnson: Who Would Win?* Minneapolis: Lerner Publications, 2024.

Wittry, Andy. *7 College Basketball Records (We Think) Will Never Be Broken.*
https://www.ncaa.com/news/basketball-men/article/2020-07-11/7-college-basketball-records-we-think-will-never-be-broken

INDEX

PHOTO ACKNOWLEDGMENTS

Photo Credits: Interior; Mtsaride/Shutterstock, interior; robertsrob/ iStockphoto, interior; Yummybuum/Shutterstock, interior; Alex Voylokov/Shutterstock, p. 4; Jamie Schwaberow/Getty, p. 5; Jeff Zelevansky/Getty, p. 7; Stock Montage/Getty, p. 8; Rich Clarkson/Getty, p. 9; Bettman/Getty, p. 10; Michael Reaves/Getty, p. 11; Media News Group/Getty, p. 12; John Biever/Getty, p. 13; Chuck Solomon/Getty, p. 14; Heinz Kluetmeier/Getty; p. 15; Bettman/Getty. p. 16; Rich Clarkson/Getty, p. 17; Bettman/Getty, p. 18; Rob Gauthier/Getty, p. 19; John Cordes/Getty, p. 20; Tony Tomsic/Getty, p. 21; John Iacono/Getty, p. 22; Bob Rosato/Getty, p. 23; Bob Rosato/Getty, p. 24; Sporting News/ Getty, p. 25; Focus on Sport/Getty, p. 26; Richard Clarkson/Getty, p. 27; Doug Hoke/Getty.

Cover: Alonzo Adams/AP